THAT'S WHAT YOU THINK!

A MIND-BOGGLING GUIDE TO THE BRAIN

LITTLE
Gestalten

CONTENT

6 A peek inside your head
Cool facts about your amazing brain

32 Bright sparks
How fast, how much and how freely we can think

58 Work those neurons!
How your brain can change

72 Every step you take
How your brain controls your body

82   Perfectly packaged
How your brain is protected and what happens if something does go wrong

100   Closed due to overcrowding?
How we remember things and how we forget

122   Listen up!
Where language comes from and how games can change your brain

140   I need sugar!
How your brain is involved in the food you eat and how it gets the energy and nutrients it needs

154   Gut feeling
When your brain doesn't get a say

168   And it was all just a dream …
What your brain gets up to at night

182   The making of
Behind the scenes at the photo shoot

A PEEK INSIDE YOUR HEAD

COOL FACTS ABOUT YOUR AMAZING BRAIN

Why are brains all wrinkly?

Brains do look quite like walnuts, don't they? In fact, the wrinkles that you can see on a brain are just a few millimetres thick. They make up the outermost layer of the brain, which is called the cerebral cortex. Those are both Latin words: "cerebral" describes things that have to do with the brain, and "cortex" means "tree bark"—quite fitting for the coating that keeps our brain under wraps, don't you think? Anyway, if we didn't have this cerebral cortex, we wouldn't be able to do a lot of the things that humans do so well: thinking, learning, feeling, reading, tasting, hearing, speaking and loads more stuff besides. Because humans can do so much, we have a bigger cerebral cortex than most other animals. To make sure our big brains can still fit in our small skulls, nature puts folds in the cortex, which is where those walnutty wrinkles come from. It's like when you have a big beach towel that you have to crumple up before it will fit in your bag.

What does a brain feel like?

It depends. The human brain is covered in three membranes (meninges), which protect it, anchor it inside the skull, and keep it supplied with blood. Although these membranes vary in thickness, they all feel quite leathery.
But if you were to remove them and run your hand over the surface of the brain itself, it would feel smooth and a bit soft. Similar to a ripe plum.

What's grey matter?

If someone tells you to "use your grey matter", they want you to switch your brain on and start thinking. The matter they're talking about refers to a greyish substance in your brain that contains neurons and nerve fibres. Neurons are the building blocks of the brain. They're cells made up of tiny fluid-filled sacs that have really long protrusions (the nerve fibres) with lots of offshoots going in all different directions. A good way to imagine neurons and nerve fibres is to think of a leafless tree with masses of branches.
But neurons aren't the only cells inside our brain. Glia cells, for instance, surround the neurons, look after them and make sure they stay the right shape. Then there are cells that are responsible for getting blood to where it has to go and for fighting off unwelcome guests like bacteria. It takes a lot of effort to keep our brain going, which is why we have so many brain cells: for every neuron we've got upstairs, there are more than two other cells working away alongside them.

How many neurons are in a brain?

Think of all the people you know, from your school bus driver all the way up to your family and closest friends. Now think of all the towns and cities you've visited, and all the people you've seen at places like trains stations and football stadiums. That's starting to sound like a lot, right? Even so, there is still no way they could ever come close to outnumbering the neurons in your head. Each of us has somewhere between 50 and 100 billion of them—that's more than all the people living on the planet! It's impossible to count that many neurons one by one, so we just have to estimate.

If you're still finding it hard to visualise those gigantic numbers, try imagining that neurons are the size of hazelnuts, and that one day we decide to fill your school with hazelnuts. Okay, it might get us in trouble with your teachers, but just focus on this for now: the number of nuts that we stuffed into the classrooms, corridors, staff room and dining hall would be similar to the number of neurons you carry around in your head every day.

How much does a brain weigh?

The human brain weighs about 1,400 grams. That's roughly the same as a big bottle of water or six apples. It's impossible to give an exact figure because (just like any part of our body and any of our organs) everyone's brain is a bit different. What we do know, though, is that *your* brain is already as heavy as an adult's. In a way, that's a lot for you to be carrying at this early stage of your life, but seeing as your brain only makes up a small fraction of your total body weight, you're more than capable of walking around with your head held high.

What colour is a brain?

From the outside, it's greyish with a hint of red. The grey comes from your grey matter (no, really?!), as well as from other brain cells. The red comes from the dense network of tiny blood vessels that keep our neurons supplied with oxygen and nutrients. You only get properly grey brains in ants and other insects, as their blood either isn't red or they don't have any blood vessels in their brain.

The inside of a brain is almost completely white. It's full of the cables (nerve fibres) that connect the different parts of the brain with each other. Just like electrical cables, the nerve fibres are covered in an insulating material. But while plastic coatings do the job for real cables, myelin is what you find on nerve fibres. Myelin is mostly made up of fat, and that fat is... wait for it... white!

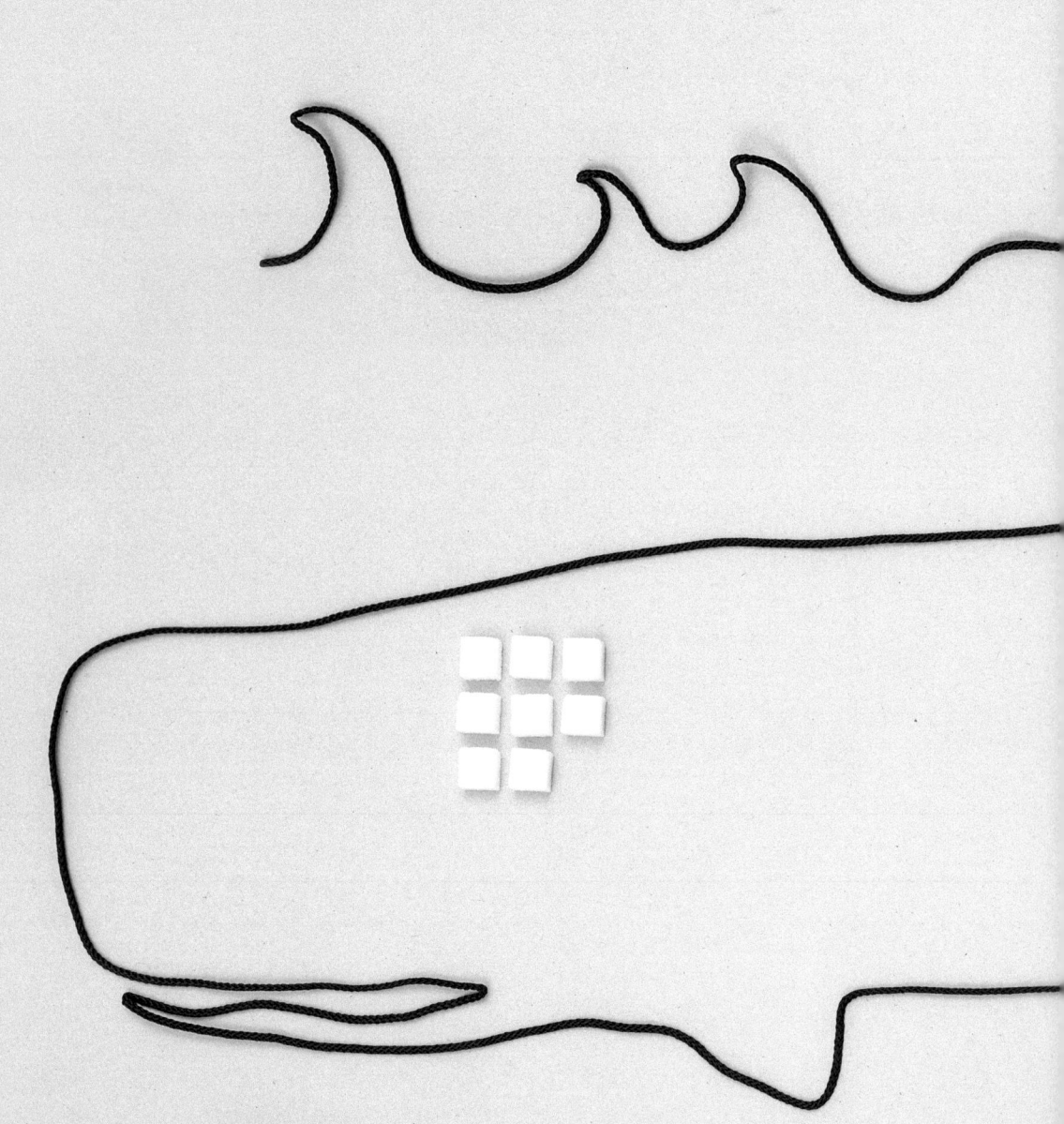

Which animal has the biggest brain?

The sperm whale holds that record. Its brain is the size of a pumpkin and weighs more than eight kilograms. That makes it five times heavier than the human version. Next in line are other types of whale (like the blue whale), and the elephant, whose brain weighs nearly five kilograms. Humans aren't too far behind, coming in at over a kilogram. The great apes (like gorillas and chimpanzees) are the Einsteins of the animal kingdom but their brains are only about half as heavy as ours. Dogs have around 100 grams stored in their heads, which is about the weight of a big bar of chocolate. Cats are down at 30 grams, and a mouse brain weighs less than one gram, which puts it on a par with a pea. The smallest brains of all weigh less than a thousandth of a gram. A housefly, for instance, has a brain that weighs just half a thousandth of a gram (although it still manages to pack in several thousand neurons). Worms come right down at the bottom of the list. At around a millionth of a gram, their extremely basic brain could be confused with a speck of dust.

Where does the word "brain" come from?

Way, way back in the days when people still spoke Old English (between the fifth and twelfth centuries), the word they used for the stuff inside their heads was "braegen". The relationship to today's word is pretty clear from that. But like a lot of English words, "brain" also has ancestors in other countries. For instance, Middle Low German (a language used from about 1100) had the word "bregen" in its vocabulary. If we look even further back in history, we get to the Ancient Greeks, who talked about their "brekhmos", which meant "forehead". So, our word "brain" is a mixture of lots of different words from lots of different places.

BOY BRAIN

Are men's and women's brains the same size?

Men's brains are actually slightly bigger than women's and weigh about 100 grams more. But before you start feeling smug (boys) or at a disadvantage (girls), consider this: even though a woman's brain is smaller, it contains more synapses than a man's brain does. Synapses are the connections that allow neurons to pass messages to each other. So is it better to have a larger brain or one that's very well connected? You'll have to decide that for yourself because, right now, scientists can only tell us three things: that women can do some things better than men, that men can do some things better than women, and that men and women are equally intelligent.

Are there any animals that don't have a brain?

Of all the animals, sponges are probably the only ones who can get by without any neurons. Sponges are really basic creatures. They don't move and they get their nourishment from things that just happen to be passing close by. If you live like that, you don't need any neurons. However, it doesn't take much for them to become a necessity: just one step up the developmental ladder brings us to jellyfish and starfish, both of which have neurons and very simple nervous systems. This allows them to react to their surroundings and make basic decisions like whether to flee or go in search of food.

Clusters of neurons located at the front of an animal—in other words, a brain—only start to show up once you get to worms. Every animal more sophisticated than a worm also has a brain: insects, birds, fish, amphibians and mammals (that includes humans, as we're also mammals).

Then there are single-celled organisms like the paramecium and the amoeba, which biologists don't class as animals. Even though they don't have any neurons, these unicellular life forms can still react to their environment. Different parts of the cell can sense things like warmth and light, and can then use that information to trigger movement.

How many wrinkles does an ant brain have?

None at all. The technical term for the ridges visible on a brain is "gyri" (one ridge is called a "gyrus"). These only develop if the cerebral cortex has to fold itself up. An ant brain is very basic and doesn't even have a cerebral cortex. It also contains fewer than a million neurons, which means it fits easily into the ant's head. Nature doesn't step in and perform its space-saving folding trick until an animal has a huge amount of neurons that have to fit inside a cerebral cortex *and* a small head.

Frogs and lizards are among the simplest animals to have a cerebral cortex. However, the outermost layer of the brain only really becomes useful for complicated things like language and thinking once we get to mammals like mice, dogs, whales and, of course, humans. They all have a big cerebral cortex, which means some of them have gyri. Mice and rats actually don't, but monkeys, whales and elephants all have a very wrinkly brain.

How long can a neuron be?

Pretty long. Think about when you stub your toe: it's painful because a neuron in your toe senses that you've banged it into something and transmits the information to your brain. That whole journey, from foot to brain, is covered by a single neuron with really long nerve fibres. Seeing as some people can be over two metres tall, a human neuron can reach nearly two metres in length. But we're not the biggest animals around by far. Take whales, for instance. Their neurons are set up in a very similar way to ours, which means it's safe to assume that they've got neurons running all the way from the tip of their tail to the top of their head. That would mean that a single blue whale neuron can probably stretch as far as 40 metres.

BRIGHT SPARKS

HOW FAST, HOW MUCH AND HOW FREELY WE CAN THINK

Did Albert Einstein have a bigger brain than everyone else?

No, it wasn't especially big—and in any case, human brains never differ much in size, and the dimensions don't play any part in deciding our intelligence. What's more, thorough studies of his brain failed to find anything else unusual about it, so perhaps Einstein hit the nail on the head when he said, "I have no special talent. I am only passionately curious." His thirst for knowledge could very well be the reason behind his achievements.

Incidentally, Einstein wasn't good at everything. As a child it took him a long time to learn to speak, he later got pretty average marks in French at school, and he never really developed the ability to see things from other people's point of view.

In the animal world, though, brain size does affect intelligence. Basically, animals with bigger brains can do more. A mouse can do more than an ant, and a dog can do more than a mouse. But there's an exception to every rule: a horse has a bigger brain than a chimpanzee but is a lot less intelligent.

ONE BUILDING SET

THREE DIFFERENT BRAINS

If we've all got the same kind of brain, why don't we all think alike?

Take a moment to think about your best friend. Even though you might have a lot of things in common, chances are you're probably both very different people. This is because everything we do, think and feel changes the connections (synapses) between our neurons and gradually alters the structure of our brain. No two people have exactly the same experiences, read exactly the same books, hear exactly the same sounds or think exactly the same thoughts. So although any two brains will look the same from the outside, they're sure to be very different on the inside.

You might think babies have identical brains because they haven't had much time to experience things yet. But in actual fact, brain differences exist right from the very start. Our parents' genes set out the basic design of our bodies. Everyone has a nose, sure, but not every nose looks alike. It's the same story with our brain. One baby might be born with a brain that's capable of making her much more intelligent than all the other babies born in that hospital on the same day. However, that doesn't automatically mean we've got another Einstein on our hands. A brain will only live up to its full potential if its owner uses it well.

In a sense, it's as if your brain is a set of building blocks. Everyone starts out with blocks that are similar, though not identical. What you build with your blocks will be different to what your friend builds. And the only way to build something amazing is to work really hard at it.

How fast can you think?

Even though it might not always seem that way, your brain often thinks faster than a car or train travelling at high speed. Neurons use electrical signals (nerve impulses) to communicate. When one neuron delivers a message to another, the signal travels along the nerve fibre at up to 220 miles per hour. That's fast, but wait till you hear this: in some of the individual sections of the nerve fibre, the signals actually reach the speed of light—that's 186,000 miles per second! Weirdly, though, it can still take a long time to work out the answer to a tricky maths problem (like multiplying 17 by 23) or to decide whether to have pizza or pasta when you're out for dinner. Your neurons might be sending messages zipping through your brain at top speed, but that's not the end of the story. When signals cross a synapse (the junction between two neurons), the neuron that receives them has to decide whether or not to pass the message on. Before it can do that, it has to add up all the signals it receives, which takes time. The delay might only be a few thousandths of a second in each case, but if a lot of neurons are involved, it can soon build up to a second or more.

Have we got different neurons for each school subject?

There's no such thing as a maths neuron—even if you're a whizz at maths, you won't have one. Getting the answer right isn't the job of one lonely cell. The secret to success lies in your neurons being able to work well in a team.

Neurons that collaborate on a particular kind of job usually live close together. This means we have a rough idea of where certain tasks are processed in the brain. For instance, the front part of your cerebral cortex (the bit just behind your forehead) is responsible for solving problems that come about when you interact with other people. The part that's towards the back of your head deals with sight, and the bit just in front of your ears handles movement.

So what about maths? Well, whenever you start grappling with an equation, the neurons that sit roughly under the headband of your headphones start firing. But because you also have to read the problem and then write down the answer, lots of other parts of your brain have to get involved too. Basically, every subject you study at school needs input from all over your brain.

Can plants think?

Plants are actually pretty intelligent. For one thing, they can react to external stimuli. Meat-eating Venus flytraps snap shut when an insect lands on them, the mimosa's leaves fold up and droop if you touch them, and flowers grow towards the light.

But despite these impressive skills, plants don't have neurons, and researchers haven't yet found any other kind of cell in them that works like a neuron. Of course, we can't rule out the possibility that plants contain things we don't understand or even know about yet. Perhaps their ability to react to their surroundings relies on a system that's entirely different to the one humans and animals use. However, we do know that plants don't have anything as complex as a brain, which means they definitely can't think, experience emotions or feel pain.

Is a brain like a computer?

Before we can answer that, we'll have to look at how brains and computers work. At the most basic level, a computer is a machine that uses a program to turn an input into an output. In other words, a computer receives pieces of information, adds them up and then uses the result to spit out something new. A brain can do that too. Say you're playing football: when the ball comes into your line of sight, the image goes through your eyes and into your brain. Once your brain has summed up all the data from the picture, it issues a command to your muscles, telling them to move so you can kick the ball. In this sense, your brain is definitely working like a computer. But unlike a computer, your brain is capable of independent learning. It can adapt to new tasks and keep pace with the changes you go through life. Whenever you find yourself in an entirely new and unexpected situation, your brain can get to grips with it. Computers can't do that because their programs are far less flexible than our grey matter is.

That's probably the biggest difference between a brain and a computer, but there are also lots of others. Computers think in binary code, which is basically a whole lot of zeroes and ones. Our brain can think on many more levels than that, which means it can process much more information than a computer can. Oh, and a brain uses fluid-filled cells to do its job, not electronic components.

How many things can you think about at once?

Our brain is an incredibly talented thing. It has loads of difficult jobs to do, and it does them all at once! It processes the sounds we hear and the images we see. It controls our blood pressure, makes sure our heart beats as it should and keeps us breathing in and out. On top of that, it moves our legs, rolls our eyes and does all kinds of other stuff besides. Experts say that the brain has to perform more than a thousand completely different tasks at any one time. If we had to actively think to get all those things done, we'd surely forget something really important on the list. Breathing would be an especially bad one to overlook... Fortunately for us, our brain has something called "consciousness", which is a wonderful thing. Apart from the brain tasks that we don't notice at all (like how it controls our organs), we are only ever really aware of one thing at a time. Don't believe us? Then ask yourself what sounds you heard while you were reading this answer.

Can neuroscientists read minds?

You've probably heard of a lie detector, right? It's a machine that measures a person's blood pressure and pulse to see if they're telling the truth or not. Film directors and authors like to put them in their detective stories so the characters can find out who committed the crime. Neuroscientists are doing something vaguely similar when they use sophisticated technology to measure activity in different parts of the brain. The results allow them to make pretty accurate predictions about which way people will go when faced with simple decisions, such as whether to raise their hand or not. Doing that is a bit like watching someone in the sweet aisle at the supermarket, though. You don't need any clever devices to work out that the bag of sweets they look at most often is probably the one that they'll end up buying. Brain researchers don't have much more insight into our thoughts than that. What's more, because each of us has a totally unique brain, there isn't much chance, even in the distant future, of people being able to listen in on our thoughts as if they were a podcast you could just download every week.

How many gigabytes of data can fit in a brain?

You can't really calculate how powerful your brain is in computer terms because it stores information in a completely different way to your laptop. But let's give it a try anyway! We'll start with a bit of background: as you know, computers store everything in bits. A bit is a single unit of information that comes in one of two values: 0 or 1, low voltage or high. A byte is usually a group of eight bits, and a gigabyte is roughly a billion bytes. Now, if we assume that every synapse between two neurons is a bit, and that our brain has 100 billion synapses, then it can store over 10,000 gigabytes (or 10 terabytes) of information. Other calculations put the figure at as much as 1,000 terabytes. That's the size of a huge library with several thousand books on its shelves, or the combined disk space of a stack of modern computers. The upshot of all of this is that you can stash away loads of information before the hard drive in your head gets anywhere near full up.

Is it true that we only use five percent of our brain?

This is a common myth. Someone probably dreamed it up as a way of getting people to buy things (books, devices, pills) that promised to boost their brain power. In fact, the very opposite is true: we use pretty much all of our brain. For one thing, whenever scientists investigate our upstairs neurons, they almost never find any that sit around doing nothing the whole time. For another, we know that nature hates waste, so if we only used very few neurons, we wouldn't have such big brains. Plus, when someone has an accident that damages parts of their brain, it almost always reduces the brain's ability to do things. That wouldn't be the case if we just used five percent of it. Basically, it's high time we forgot about this odd little fairy tale. What is true, though, is that we don't use all our neurons at the same time. Different tasks need action from different parts of the brain. It wouldn't be very efficient to activate them all at once. When you're reading a book, for instance, there's not much point in your brain worrying about making your legs move or helping you speak.

Can you control someone's brain by planting thoughts in it?

We humans are basically free to think what we like. However, experiments on mice have shown that it is possible to turn neurons on and off from outside the brain. The scientists who conducted the study made some of the neurons in each mouse's brain sensitive to light. They then used super-thin fibre-optic cables to shine light into the brain. When the light hit the neurons with the light sensors, it activated them and they changed the mouse's behaviour. The mouse would run in circles, for instance, or suddenly become less timid. The scientists hope their findings will eventually be able to help treat sick people.

That's obviously a pretty complicated experiment, but you don't need to be a high-flying researcher to influence other people's thoughts. To see what we mean, try this simple trick. Ask your friend to say the word "white" ten times. As soon as she's finished, ask her what cows drink. If she says "milk", you've managed to outsmart her brain. We all connect the words "white" and "cow" with the word "milk", so when you send them both whizzing around her brain and ask her what cows drink, it's pretty likely she'll come up with the wrong answer. If you want to avoid giving the first answer that pops into your head, you have to concentrate and think hard.

WORK THOSE NEURONS!

HOW YOUR BRAIN CAN CHANGE
Is it possible to train your brain?

You mean like sport for grey matter? Sure, that exists. Everything (and we mean everything) that you do gives your brain a workout and ends up changing it. If you spend a long time working hard at something, and hopefully enjoying it, then you'll end up being really good at it. The more you practise, the better your synapses get at doing their job for that particular skill. Sometimes your brain even puts extra neurons to work to help you on your way. It's almost as if you're building up muscles in your head. But practising one thing all the time won't change your whole brain. Think about athletes. Their biggest, most toned muscles are the ones that they need for their chosen sport. It's the same with the brain—the muscles develop in the parts we train the most. If we focus on learning poems by heart, then our memory gets better. If we spend hours playing computer games, then our reaction times speed up. On the flip side, whenever we stop doing something, the synapses we needed for that skill get weaker and disappear. This is why our brain stays the same size no matter how much exercise it gets.

When it comes to cerebral sport, being an all-rounder is the best bet. If you want to avoid becoming someone with amazing reaction times but a dreadful memory, poor motor skills and difficulties communicating, then you need to vary your activities and practise lots of different things. Read books, do sport, play computer games, make music, climb a mountain… you'll have great fun and your brain will love you for it.

Were people in the Stone Age cleverer than us?

"Homo sapiens" is the scientific name for us, the species of human that still walks the Earth today. We were also alive back in the Stone Age, but at that time our brain was smaller than the one we have now and not much bigger than the one found in great apes. That means we must be more intelligent than our Stone Age ancestors were. Still, some people might argue that humans today aren't actually that clever, seeing as so many of them are intent on destroying the environment and each other. This would also mean that, as a species, we're not doing so well at living up to the name "Homo sapiens", which translates roughly (and not very modestly) as "wise man".

Incidentally, Homo sapiens wasn't alone during the Stone Age. Other humans, known as Neanderthals, also existed back then and their brain was the same size as the one we have now, perhaps even a bit larger. Yet despite having more brain space than Homo sapiens, the Neanderthals were the ones that ended up going extinct. Why did that happen? Maybe they couldn't speak and so couldn't communicate with each other while out hunting. Perhaps they died from a disease they caught from Homo sapiens. Or maybe they needed more food than Homo sapiens did, which meant they couldn't get enough nourishment during the Ice Age. Right now, it's a mystery. Perhaps you'll be the one to solve it some day.

When did brains start to appear in animal evolution?

Next time you come across an earthworm, take a moment to examine it. It looks pretty simple from the outside—no arms, no legs and nothing like a head. Even so, you can easily tell which end is the front when it starts moving. As it crawls along, the worm stretches out at the front, which means that's the part that comes into contact with food and threats first. Because of this, the ancestors of today's earthworm started to evolve in a way that put most of their sensory cells and nerves at the front end of their body. Those simple brains began appearing over 600 million years ago. Once nature realised it had hit on a good idea, it stuck with it and the design has stood the test of time.

Do you have a brain before you're born?

Yes. The brain starts developing just after the sperm has fertilised the egg. Three weeks into a pregnancy, cells start to form a tube that will later produce all the neurons for the baby's brain, spinal cord and body. Once it exists, the tube keeps on growing and changing. At two months, you can see bulges starting to form at the front end of the tube. These are known as the primary brain vesicles and will later develop into the brain itself. As the pregnancy continues, the brain becomes more and more recognisable and can do more and more things. By the fourth month, the visual system is so well developed that the foetus (the unborn baby) reacts to light. By the sixth month, it can hear what's going on outside. And that's not all. Because a brain is such a clever thing, babies can have a whale of a time while they're in the womb. They can sleep whenever they like, suck their thumb and even do somersaults!

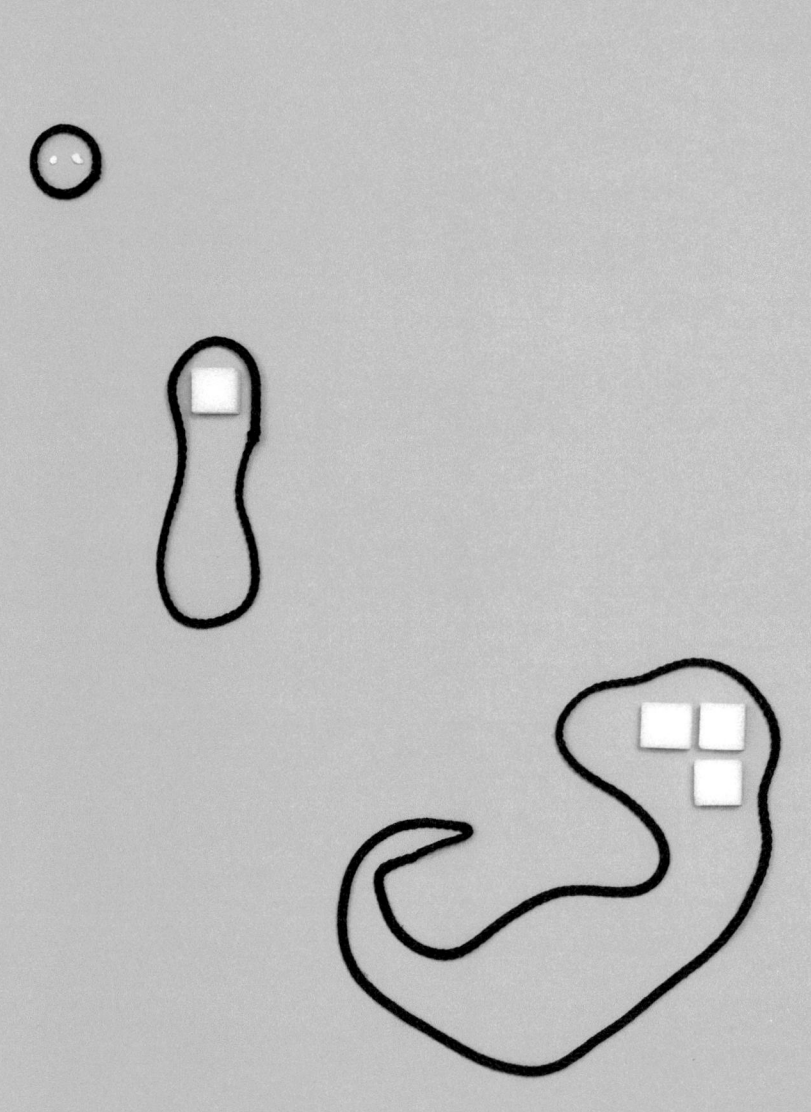

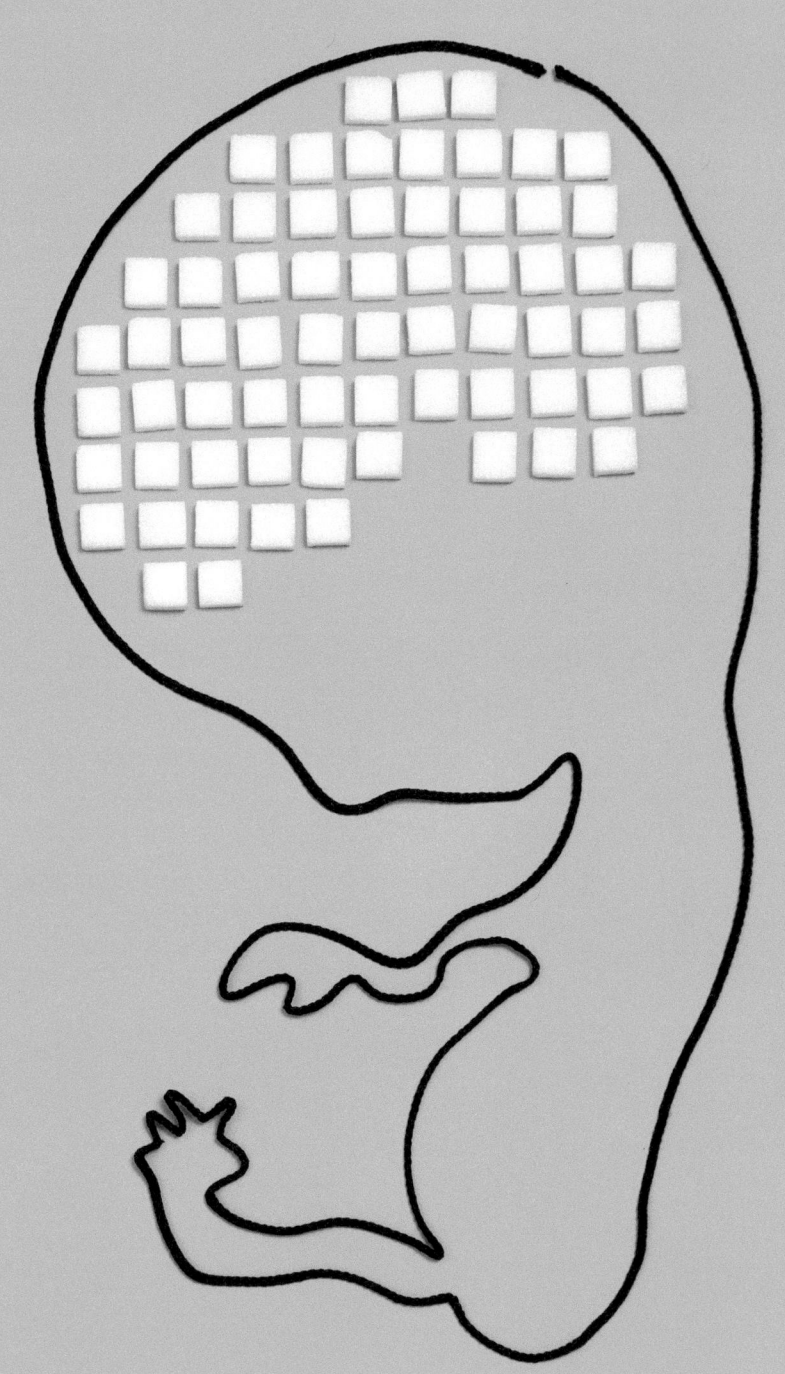

How big is a baby's brain when it's born?

A newborn's brain weighs about 300 grams, which is roughly a quarter the weight of an adult brain. Even so, it contains almost all the neurons the baby will ever need. The reason it weighs so little is that, in the same way as a sapling starts out all skinny and with just a few branches, the baby's neurons are still really small and the nerve fibres don't have many offshoots. Not long after the birth, though, the baby's synapses start developing and its neurons gradually get bigger. That obviously makes the brain heavier, and it keeps growing until it weighs more than four times as much as it did at the start.

Is my brain still growing?

Outwardly, your brain is fully grown. Inwardly, it's still basically one big construction site. The whole thing works like this: once you're born, the number of synapses that connect your neurons together grows at top speed. A three-year-old has twice as many synapses as an adult does. The difference is that a child's neurons work really slowly because the nerve fibres aren't very well insulated yet. But over the years that changes. The fibres get better insulated and the brain can start to function much faster. Most of this has already happened by the time you get to your age. The next big changes come when you hit puberty and your brain embarks on a huge clean-up operation. It gets rid of unnecessary synapses and straightens out crooked pathways so that it can think without having to make so many detours. What a bright idea.

EVERY STEP

HOW YOUR BRAIN CONTROLS YOUR BODY

How much of my body is connected to my brain?

Your brain is your body's control centre. Nothing works without it. If it disappeared, you wouldn't be able to feel anything and you'd hardly be able to move. That's why pretty much everything in our body is hooked up to our brain. Nerve fibres connect the neurons in our brain and spinal cord to all our limbs and organs. The fibres that are linked to our muscles, for instance, allow us to move our arms, legs, fingers and toes. But control-centre neurons don't do their job alone. We have other neurons and cells distributed throughout our body that keep watch over everything that's happening and make sure that the brain is up to date. So if our arm bends, if someone or something touches our skin, if a picture comes into our line of sight, or if we hear a noise, those other neurons and cells sense it and pass the information back to the brain. They also tell the brain about things we aren't consciously aware of, like our blood pressure and blood sugar levels. Once the brain gets that information, it uses its connections to the relevant organs to tell them whether to work harder or ease off.

Could a brain ever grow bigger than a head?

In a way, your brain is already bigger than your head. That sounds a bit mad, but let us explain. A big part of your nervous system—the spinal cord—isn't located in your head, but inside your spine. As well as connecting your brain to the rest of your body, the spinal cord also triggers your reflexes. One example of a reflex is when the doctor taps your knee with that little hammer and it makes your leg jolt. Reflexes help you with standing and walking because they automatically keep a low level of tension in your muscles. Without that, your muscles would be too limp to keep you upright and you'd end up on the floor. Reflexes also protect you. For instance, they'll make you pull your hand away really fast if you touch a hotplate. The neat thing about reflexes is that they don't need any input from you: they work all by themselves.

Why does our brain control movement?

Because it's the expert. Have you ever tried to teach someone younger than you to ride a bike? If so, you'll know that it's *really* difficult. What do you get them to do first? Steer, peddle, brake? And then there's the small matter of balance—how in the world do you explain how to do that?! The funny thing is, after a while, riding a bike gets really easy. It just takes a bit of practice.

Your brain controls almost all of your movements by sending orders to special nerve pathways in your spinal cord. These then transmit the information to the muscles in different parts of your body. The parts that we can use best are the ones that have the most neurons working on them in the brain. For instance, humans are really good with their hands because our brain contains lots of neurons that specialise in moving fingers. But your brain doesn't just give the orders for muscles to move—it also receives feedback from your body. Your brain knows exactly what it feels like when a movement is performed correctly, which is why your body reports back on things like how far the movement has gone, whether there are any problems and whether the movement needs to be adjusted. These messages are issued by the sensory cells in your muscles, joints and skin. The information travels through the spinal cord and back to the brain, in the opposite direction to the command that told the muscles to move in the first place.

As well as the movements that we consciously want to make, our brain can also trigger movements that we hardly even notice. They're the ones that help us do things like stay balanced once we've mastered the art of riding a bike.

How does the brain send commands around my body?

Using electricity, mostly. Each neuron can generate a tiny current and send small electrical signals whizzing along its nerve fibres. But those alone won't make us move. For that to happen, we need to add muscles to the mix. When the nerve fibre delivers its signal to a muscle cell, the electricity causes the cell to contract. When lots of muscle cells all contract at once, the whole muscle gets shorter and, hey presto, your arm or leg moves. To see this in action, stretch one arm out straight and look at your biceps (the muscle at the top of your arm). Right now it's long and sort of flat. But if you bend your arm up at the elbow, you'll see it get shorter and fatter.

Does a part of your brain die if you become paraplegic?

No, but just like your whole life changes if you have an accident that leaves you paraplegic, so your brain has to make some major adjustments. A paraplegic person can no longer walk or stand, but they need to use their arms in a whole new way so that they can get around in a wheelchair. The brain reacts to this by giving new jobs to the parts of it that used to make the person stand, walk, and feel things in their legs. It's quite simple, really: the neurons that used to do one thing just end up doing another. However, some neurons can die off if too much of their nerve fibre was severed in the accident.

PERFECTLY PACKAGED

HOW YOUR BRAIN IS PROTECTED AND WHAT HAPPENS IF SOMETHING DOES GO WRONG

Why is our brain round and not square?

We humans seem to like right angles. Lego bricks have them, exercise books have them, and so do windows and houses. Nature sees things differently. You'll almost never find a right angle on a flower, a tree or an animal. That's because nature always chooses the shape that's best suited to the job, and there are very few instances where a sharp corner beats everything else.

But there's another reason why our brain is rounded. If you drop a box, the corners will get crushed and crumpled really easily. But a spherical object (as long as we're not talking about porcelain) is much less likely to end up damaged. A rounded brain and a domed skull are therefore sturdier and better able to withstand bumps. In some cases, though, our natural defences aren't enough and we need extra protection. That's why people wear helmets for things like cycling and skiing.

Could you use someone else's brain to cure a person who's brain dead?

Organ transplants are amazing things. If someone's kidney stops working, then as long as doctors can find a donor kidney that matches the patient, they can use it to replace the faulty one and save a life. Lots of organs are transplantable these days—kidneys, heart, lungs, liver, pancreas, to name just a few. Unfortunately, the brain isn't on that list. It would be impossible to perform the operation because the brain is connected to the body via millions and millions of nerve fibres. If doctors did try to transplant one, first they'd have to work out what should be linked to what, and then reconnect everything. Even if they could find and join up each nerve fibre in ten seconds, the operation would still last several years.

Another problem is that neurons in the brain die really quickly if they're not properly looked after. Just one minute without a blood supply will cause them to stop working. And what do you think the chances are of getting a donor brain ready for transplant in under a minute?

Can our brain repair damaged neurons or grow new ones?

If you cut yourself, the wound usually closes up within a few days because your skin cells start growing back. While neurons can also get damaged through injury or illness, they can't repair themselves so easily. We're born with almost all the neurons we'll ever have, and although our brain does grow some new ones during our lives, it's not many and it only happens in certain parts of our brain. Also, neurons find it extremely difficult to rebuild the connection to their nerve fibres if they get severed in an accident. The process can go really slowly, and if the fibre is too long then the neuron can't restore the link at all. Researchers are working hard to solve the problem and have already succeeded in making fibres and neurons grow back together in mice.

Unlike us, though, some animals have the remarkable ability to repair their neurons very well indeed. Our inability to do so is probably the price we have to pay for having such a powerful brain. If we started growing lots of new neurons, they might mess up the super-complex networks that already exist in our heads.

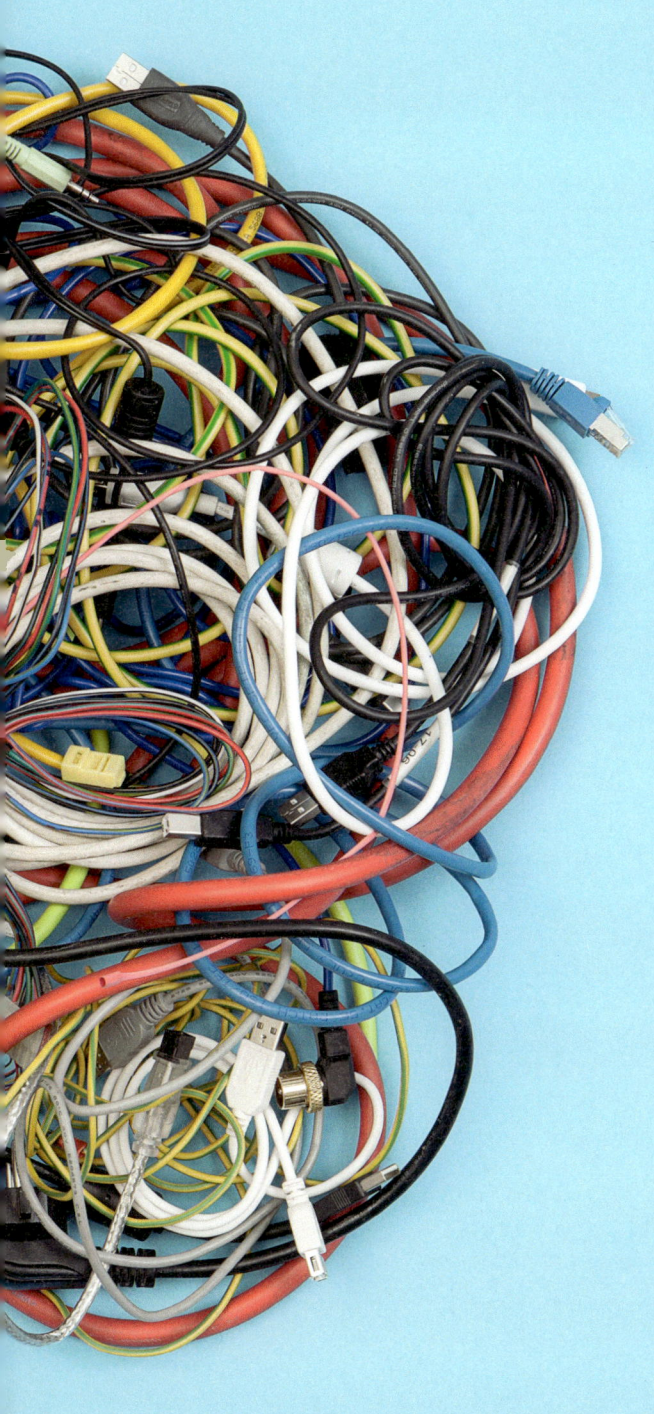

Is our brain hollow?

Far from it. The cerebral cortex is full of neurons, each of which is connected to several thousand other neurons by a long nerve fibre. This dense network takes up almost all the space inside your brain.

However, we do have some small hollow areas in there. They're called ventricles and are filled with a clear liquid known as cerebrospinal fluid. It's only a little bit, though—no more than half a glass of the stuff.

Cerebrospinal fluid also exists outside the brain, where it acts as a bumper between the soft tissue of our brain and the hard bone of our skull. To get an idea of how that works, take a hard rubber ball into the swimming pool. Try throwing it against the wall underwater and you'll see that you can't throw it nearly as hard as you can on dry land.

Can your brain get hot?

If something gets us really angry, we might say it made steam come out of our ears. But even though anger can make us feel all hot and bothered, our brain's temperature doesn't actually rise. We just feel as if it does because, without noticing, we start to tense our muscles and get a bit sweaty and red in the face, as if we're running the 100 metres. It's sort of our brain's way of telling us to take a step back from the conflict and relax. So what happens if we decide to stand our ground and keep arguing? Nothing: our brain still won't heat up. No matter what you're doing—snoozing, watching TV, puzzling over your homework or shouting at your parents or little brother—your brain's temperature never changes. That's because you're always using roughly the same amount of neurons, so your grey matter always uses roughly the same amount of energy.

That said, some things *can* make your brain get hot. If you stay out in the sun too long without a hat, for instance, the heat will irritate the meninges that surround your brain. This causes a painful condition known as sunstroke. If you insist on continuing to sunbathe even after that's happened, the meninges can become really inflamed and totally ruin your holiday.

What happens when you get a headache?

For a start, your head throbs like crazy and you'd do anything for a magic wand to make the pain go away. But directing the wand at your brain would do no good. Your brain has no pain receptors, which means it can't actually feel pain and so isn't directly responsible for your misery. What often causes headaches are the meninges that surround the brain, and the blood vessels. They contain nerve fibres that tell the brain when they are being irritated or stretched. The brain then translates those messages into something that feels really unpleasant: pain. So if your meninges swell up because you've been out in the sun too long, or if your nerve fibres get stretched because you've taken a serious bang to the head, your brain sounds the alarm and hopes that the pain will make you stop whatever it is you're doing.

Headaches aren't always so complicated, though. Sometimes you can get one just from standing or sitting in a weird way, from wearing your ponytail too tight, or from being stressed and angry. In those cases, your brain works out that something's not right with your head, and signals it by giving you a headache.

Can you bruise your brain if you bang your head against a wall?

Thankfully, an accident like that usually just results in a lump or a bruise on your head. But if you were to crash into a wall at top speed, your brain might end up banging against the inside of your skull, or your skull might break and the bone fragments could lodge in your brain. The absolute worst-case scenario would be that neurons become severed from their nerve fibres. A major bang to the head can also cause blood vessels to rupture, sending blood into the brain and damaging lots of neurons. A lump or bruise on your forehead will disappear with no lasting problems, but because it's practically impossible for your brain to repair neurons, a more serious accident can lead to permanent brain damage.

What happens if you get a concussion?

Imagine a factory gets hit by an earthquake. Everything inside the building will end up in a big mess and it will take a while for the factory to sort itself out and start working properly again. It's the same with your brain. A heavy blow to the head will shake up your neurons and make it hard for them to do their job. When a lot of neurons struggle to function, your whole brain suffers. You'll feel drowsy and dizzy, your head will hurt and you'll feel sick into the bargain. Scientists don't exactly know if this causes any real damage to the brain. Although a concussion will heal itself within a few days and without any long-term problems, it also sends substances into the blood that should really only be in the neurons. So if you feel ill for longer than a few days, or if you notice that you're having other problems, you should make an appointment with your doctor.

CLOSED DUE TO OVERCROWDING?

HOW WE REMEMBER THINGS AND HOW WE FORGET

Does our memory work like a camera?

Nope. When you take a photo, the camera records everything it sees, right down to the smallest detail. But when your eyes transmit an image to your brain, only a fraction of the information gets stored in your memory. Ideally, we remember the things, people and events that are most important to us or that surprise us by being different to what we were expecting. For instance, you might remember how, on the day you all had your family photo taken, your aunt wore a really pretty dress and your big brother was being more annoying than usual. Chances are, though, you probably won't remember what the weather was like.

Often, a memory only exists because we return to it again and again. In the case of the family photo, you might remember the day mainly because you look at the picture a lot with your parents and talk about what happened. Revisiting it like this means that you think about the day at different stages of your life. You process the events based on the experiences that you have gathered in the years since the photo was taken, and then store the memories in their revised form. This is how memories change. And because our brain usually casts us in a better light than was really the case, you might eventually forget that you were actually the one who wound your brother up in the first place.

Can anyone remember everything they see?

Chances are your classmates can't and, surprising though it might sound, your parents probably can't either. However, there are people in the world who do have amazing memory powers. Stephen Wiltshire is one of them. He has a photographic memory. After just a short flight over New York City, he was able to produce a picture of the skyline that showed all the buildings in lifelike detail. Kim Peek was another. He memorised everything he ever read, and in the end could recall the contents of more than 10,000 books.

As incredible as these abilities are, the people with them usually have serious difficulties in areas of their lives that come very easily to the rest of us. They might struggle to tell left from right, or have no awareness of other people's feelings. In this sense, a photographic memory can be considered a kind of brain disorder.

Why do you forget some things straight away?

Wouldn't it be great if you could just revise your German vocabulary once and then get 100% on the test? Funnily enough, it's actually good that our brain can't do that. An unbelievable number of things happen to us every moment of every day. We meet up with friends, chat, listen to music, smell the smell of salt & vinegar crisps, realise that we're feeling cold—all at the same time. If we remembered absolutely everything, our heads would soon be stuffed full of completely useless information.

That's why our brain only stores the things that look like they might be useful for us in the future. If you just read the vocabulary list once, your brain's never going to think it's important enough to keep hold of. Only once you read it again and again, start to like the sound of the words and begin building them into sentences will your brain decide that it's time to find some room for them. This is very efficient because it means you don't waste valuable brain space on pointless details. So the next time it takes you ages to learn an especially tricky German word, don't worry: it's a sign that your brain is working perfectly!

When I see something, how much of it do I remember?

Not very much at all. We see the equivalent of roughly a million bits of information every second, and once our brain registers an image, it takes just one more second for it to delete almost all of the information. Much less than a thousandth of the original image ends up in our short-term memory, and even then it only sticks around for a few minutes. Less than a hundredth of that (about one bit per second) gets into our long-term memory, where it stays for anything from a few days to our whole life.

Our brain therefore filters out most of what we see. To get an idea of how little remains, find yourself a thick book. Now imagine that it's taken you one second to see every letter in that book. Your short-term memory would let you remember something like half a page's worth for a few minutes, and just a single letter would end up in your long-term memory.

Can you injure your head so badly that you lose your memory?

Sort of. Some brain injuries might mean that you stop being able to recall your personal memories, like what you did on your last birthday or what happened on the day you had your accident. Think of it like a computer that can't access the data stored on its hard drive anymore. But even if the personal parts of your memory get lost, others will usually stay put, like the ones that tell you how to ride a bike or write.

In very rare cases, the inside of a patient's brain is damaged in such a way that they can remember everything that happened before the accident, but immediately forget anything new that happens to them afterwards. If you ask them who visited them in hospital that morning or what they had for lunch, they wouldn't be able to tell you. To use the computer example again, it's as if their hard drive is refusing to store any new data.

Why do people sometimes forget really bad things that happen to them?

When something so terrible happens to a person that they can't bear to think about it, they might try their hardest to remove it from their memory. If it ever starts to make an appearance in their minds, they quickly switch their thoughts to something else or start an activity that will stop them thinking about it. In really serious cases, the brain sweeps the memory away so fast that the person isn't even aware that it's happening. Even though this can make it seem like the memory doesn't exist, it is still there and will usually come back over time.

How do we store knowledge?

If we want to be sure of remembering something, we'll probably write it down or type it out. That goes for things like vocabulary (on index cards), e-mail addresses (in our smartphones) and groceries (on a shopping list). For a long time, people thought the brain worked the same way: that everything we learn is written down and stored somewhere in our grey matter, a bit like books in a library. But it turns out we were wrong. A memory doesn't exist in just one place. For us to remember something, our neurons and their synapses have to undergo a permanent change and create a chain that connects different regions of the brain. Each region is responsible for a specific task, like hearing things, feeling things or working out maths problems. To find someone in your phone book, you start by scrolling to the first letter of the person's name. That one letter leads you to their phone number, e-mail address and whatever else you've stored under their contact. Your brain is similar, in that it finds a memory by thinking of one particular part of it. Let's use a birthday party as an example. At the time, your brain might store away information like the smell of the cake, how you were feeling, and the song your mum was humming all day. When you grow up, hearing that song on the radio will be enough to bring back everything else about the party. The music wakes up part of the memory chain that your neurons created all those years ago. Once that happens, all the other parts of the chain connected to the melody also become active.

Why are elderly people so forgetful?

Our bodies change as we grow older. Skin gets wrinkly and hearts become weaker. The ageing process also affects our brain: it shrinks a bit, parts of it stop working so well, and improving or creating new synapses becomes harder. This is why older people can find it difficult to remember things. They might forget what's on the shopping list or where they've put their glasses. Handling new information is also more of a challenge, which is why elderly people can be nervous about using computers or smartphones. However, they have a huge advantage over young people when it comes to dealing with complex tasks. They've collected so much experience and built up so many memory chains over the years that they can solve problems that might seem impossible to you.

Despite the changes that age brings about, we never lose the ability to learn. For older people, the process will be slower than it was in their younger days, but their neurons are still capable of changing and creating new synapses that can store new information. The only time the human brain will really deteriorate is if you do nothing with it.

Will your brain disintegrate if you get Alzheimer's?

If an elderly person develops Alzheimer's, their brain will lose its abilities much faster than if they were to grow old without the disease. At first they will find it hard to remember things, then speaking and thinking will become more difficult. As time goes on, more and more parts of the brain will stop working, until eventually the patient dies from brain failure.

While none of this causes the brain to disintegrate, it does make it shrink. The disease kills off the synapses that connect one neuron to the other, and then destroys the neurons themselves. This deepens the grooves in the cerebral cortex and increases the size of the hollow spaces filled with cerebrospinal fluid. The brain can lose up to 300 grams in weight like this.

How long will I remember the stuff I learn in school?

You know how if you walk through a field of long grass, you can make a path that wasn't there before? The first time you do it, a lot of the grass you stomp down might spring back up once you've moved on. But walk up and down it several times, and the grass will stick to the ground for longer and you'll probably make the path wider. If, after a while, you go away and don't use the path for a long time, it will get overgrown again. You'll have to re-stomp it to bring it back, but you won't have to start from scratch because you'll still be able to roughly make out where the original path went. That, in a nutshell, is how your memory works. Once your brain has created long-term memories of the things you learn in school, your head is full of pathways made of neurons linked up like chains. The strength of the connections between the neurons depends on how often you use the stored information or how important it is to you. The stronger the connection, the easier it is to find the route again. Most of the paths stick around in some shape or form even if you don't use them very much, so it's not unusual to find that you suddenly remember things you thought you'd forgotten long ago.

Why can little kids usually remember more than grown-ups?

The human brain adapts itself to the tasks that life presents us with. When we're very young, we have to take in and retain loads of information, like how to speak, how to read, how to button a shirt, and how to look left and right before crossing the road. Almost everything is new to us when we're small, and we have to learn a lot from scratch. That's why a very young brain can pick up things so quickly and remember so much.

Once you get a bit older, you've seen and learned a lot of things. Your task is then to apply that knowledge. An adult brain has a lot of life experience, which means it (usually) finds it easier to tell the difference between information worth storing and information that should be discarded. That sounds good, but it's actually not always an advantage. If an adult is playing the Memory card game with kids, for instance, the adult is more likely to lose. That's because children pay more attention to details and soak up everything that they see. Adults always try to put things into groups, so if they turn over a card that has a dog on it, they'll remember the word "pet", not "dog". The same thing happens if they get a card with a cat on it, which explains why adults can sometimes be pretty bad at Memory.

Where do your memories go if you lose your memory?

Do you remember last Christmas? The smell of the tree, how excited you were about your presents, how yummy Christmas dinner was and how you still had room for loads of chocolates afterwards? All those memories are usually spread throughout your brain. More precisely, they're stored in different parts of your cerebral cortex.

If you lose your memory, it's usually not because your individual memories vanish into thin air. The problem is that you no longer know how to get to them. It's as if you've lost the map to your mind and can't find the streets that connect all your memories together.

If you get your memory back, it usually starts with just small islands reappearing like scraps of memories floating free in your mind. A patient might remember the smell of the Christmas tree, but not the point in time that he or she smelled it. Over time, the brain reconnects the islands, and the picture becomes whole again.

LISTEN UP!

WHERE LANGUAGE COMES FROM AND HOW GAMES CAN CHANGE YOUR BRAIN

Are both halves of our brain involved in language?

We've got two of a lot of things—two arms, two legs, two eyes, two ears—so it make sense that we've got two halves to our brain. They're each responsible for one side of our body, although not in the way you might expect: the left half controls our right side, and the right half does our left side. But language isn't an arm or a leg, so the brain deals with it differently. The left half handles most of it, which means you can understand language and speak it pretty well with no input from the right at all. However, if we didn't have the right half and if the two didn't communicate, we wouldn't be able to pick up on the subtleties of language, like intonation and puns. Lucky for us, then, that our left and right brain are very well connected.

Where does our brain store foreign languages?

Understanding spoken and written language relies on a part of the cerebral cortex that sits roughly above our left ear. But it can't do the job alone. It also needs the parts of the brain that allow us to see words and hear them, and the parts where the words are stored in our memory. That all adds up to a lot of cerebral cortex, which is why we can't really say exactly where a language is stored. But if we're talking about the simple ability to understand a language or speak it, then a foreign language occupies roughly the same spaces as our native language does. This is no great surprise, as it's perfectly in keeping with the way the brain works. Rather than store new information as never-before-seen data, our brain always tries to connect it with existing knowledge. So when we learn the German word for "dog", we just have to connect everything we already know about dogs with a new sound and a new combination of letters.

Could you ever train an ape to speak?

Now that would be something: apes reciting poems or arguing with you over who gets the last piece of chocolate. It won't ever happen, though, because apes can't make the sounds necessary for speaking our language. Also, an ape's tongue and larynx are set up differently to ours, which means they'd only ever be able to pronounce a handful of words.

But that doesn't mean apes, and in particular the great apes, can't *learn* our language. Researchers have found that chimpanzees can learn several hundred words, while some especially clever ones who practise a lot can manage more than 1,000. The reason the researchers know this is that they taught the chimps how to communicate using either sign language or a board filled with symbols that represented the words. As impressive as this is, a chatty chimp can never get close to a human's vocabulary, which usually contains tens of thousands of words.

How do the words we hear get into our head?

Drop a stone into a lake and, apart from the satisfying noise and impressive splash, you'll see that it sends waves radiating out from where it went in. When someone starts speaking, the words they say act a bit like that stone, in that they cause invisible waves to ripple through the air. When the waves reach your ear, they travel down into it until they come to a thin membrane called an eardrum. The waves make the eardrum vibrate, and then tiny bones that sit on the other side of it amplify those vibrations and transfer them to fluid in your inner ear. Once that happens, your ear has transformed airborne sound waves into real waves in a liquid. These then stimulate cells in the inner ear that act like neurons and produce electrical signals that are picked up by other neurons and transported to the brain. Every tone that we hear—from the really high ones to the really low—has its own dedicated neurons.

So far, so good. But how does our brain produce words from tones, and how can we pick our friend's voice out from all the talking and noise going on in the classroom? To work out who and what we're hearing, our brain has to do its usual trick of using lots of different neurons to collect and process lots of different information.

Can watching TV or playing computer games alter your brain?

Yes. While you sit on the couch channel-hopping or playing the latest video game, your brain is still running at top speed. Just like everything else you do, this activity changes the way your brain works. Some alterations are for the better. They'll make it easier for you to process images that appear in rapid succession, your reaction times will speed up and you'll have more precise control over your fingers and thumbs. Unfortunately, if you spend too much time in front of the TV or the computer, you're heading for all kinds of problems. This is because the synapses between the neurons in the parts of your brain that aren't getting any exercise will become weaker or disappear altogether. You'll find it harder to think, your imagination will suffer and your language skills will stagnate. On top of all that, the lack of movement will make you fat and you'll get ill more easily. The best thing to do is limit your TV and computer time to no more than an hour a day.

What happens in our brain when we read?

Reading can seem like a pretty one-sided task for the brain. You don't have to listen or feel, you hardly need to move, there's no need to make decisions and you're asking a lot less of your sight than you are when watching TV. But in fact, reading actually allows the brain to do a lot of things that it doesn't have time for when it's too busy dealing with those other tasks. It gives you space to let your imagination and creativity run wild, which is why reading is such a good way of training your brain to paint its own pictures (far better than staring at the TV).

Still, reading too much can also be harmful, as your brain will become weaker in other areas and you'll end up losing important skills, just like if you watched too much TV or spent too long playing computer games. That's why it's a good idea fill your free time with a mix of activities. Reading should ideally be one of them, and giving it about an hour a day would be brilliant.

Are games and music good for your brain?

Playing games at an adventure playground, or playing at being someone else for a theatre production both mean that you're testing out new connections in your brain that might be useful to you now and in the future. Playing lets you find out what you can do well and might give you ideas that no one's had before. Learning to play a musical instrument uses loads of different parts of your brain. Plus, you have to coordinate your movements, apply your sense of touch, and use your intuition, imagination and creativity. Of course, that does mean that it's really difficult at the start, but the good news is that it creates and strengthens connections in your brain—so much so that some scientists believe making music boosts your intelligence.

HOW YOUR BRAIN IS INVOLVED IN THE FOOD YOU EAT AND HOW IT GETS THE ENERGY AND NUTRIENTS IT NEEDS

Why is our brain in our head and not our stomach?

When nature was still working on simple animals like worms, it found that the best design solution was to put the sensory organs at the front of the body, close to the animal's mouth and facing its direction of travel. Because the idea worked so well, nature carried it over into higher animals, which meant it also wound up in humans. In short, our brain is in our head because that's where our ears, eyes and mouth are.

But that doesn't mean our bellies are entirely free of neurons. We've got about 100 million down there, as it happens. They work relatively independently of the brain and help to control our gut by making the wall of our intestines (which is where they live) contract and relax. If you've ever wondered where a stomach rumble comes from, there's your answer! The action of our gut mixes up the food we've eaten and makes it easier to digest. Once the food has been partially digested, the contractions then move it (and eventually the waste that's left after our body has absorbed all the nutrients) through our intestines.

How much blood flows through our brain?

Your heart pumps roughly four litres of blood around your body every minute, and a quarter of that goes to your brain. That's a massive amount if you think about how small your brain is compared to the rest of your body. So it's not exactly an energy-saving organ.

But why does our brain need the red stuff in the first place? Well, just like your desk lamp needs electricity, and a car needs petrol, so your brain needs energy to work. In its case, the energy comes from glucose (a form of sugar that we get from food and that our body can produce itself) and oxygen (a gas that we get by breathing air into our lungs). Blood transports both of these things to the brain. The process goes like this: once we've inhaled oxygen and eaten or produced glucose, they go into our blood. Our heart then pumps some of that blood to the brain. The blood vessels up there spread out in lots of different branches that get narrower and narrower until they're thinner than a single hair. Our neurons then absorb the oxygen and glucose and use them to produce the energy that the brain needs to function.

Why is alcohol bad for you?

Alcohol (the kind you get in things like beer, wine and spirits) is a toxin. So are the substances it produces when the body breaks it down. As well as damaging the liver, stomach and other organs, alcohol is also bad news for neurons. Once alcohol enters the body, it gets into the blood stream and travels to the brain. There, it activates what's known as the reward system and makes the person feel happy and relaxed. Sounds nice, right? But wait. If the person keeps drinking, the alcohol will start to affect the way their neurons talk to each other. The communication gradually gets weaker and weaker until the neurons can't work properly any more. This is when the person begins to stagger and slur their words. Their vision goes blurry, and it gets hard to remember things and stay in control. Eventually, the neurons begin to die off. A single drunken night can spell the end for several million of these clever little cells.

Now you're probably wondering why getting drunk would ever seem like a good idea to anyone. The trouble is, alcohol is addictive. If someone drinks a lot, the nice effects start getting weaker, which means they have to drink even more to feel as "good" as they did the first time around.

Can you eat brains?

A dish of brains wouldn't be a very good dinner choice. Although they contain similar ingredients to a cake (sugar, protein and fat), brains definitely don't taste like a homemade Victoria sponge. In fact, their fat content is so high that they taste pretty disgusting. Another reason for keeping them off the menu is that scientists believe humans who eat animal brains risk contracting serious and unusual brain diseases.

How does the food I eat affect my brain?

Of all the food you eat, your brain is especially interested in one particular type of sugar: glucose. If your body doesn't have enough of it, then your brain can't function properly. But before you jump for joy and go running to your parents to tell them they have to give you unlimited access to the biscuit tin, read on. Because glucose is so important for your brain, your body has lots of backup systems to make sure it gets just the right amount, whether you're stuffing your face with sugary treats or haven't eaten for a while. That's good news for your brain but bad news for you, as there's no need for you to up your biscuit intake, and no point in reaching for high-sugar snacks before an exam.
But although your brain doesn't really mind what you eat in the short term, it does need certain nutrients to keep functioning and developing in the long run. The same goes for the blood vessels that supply the brain. Eat a healthy, balanced diet, and your brain (as well as your body) will thank you.

Why does food taste bad when I've got a cold?

If you've ever dived into a swimming pool and had water shoot up your nose, you'll know how unpleasant it is when it gets into your throat or, more specifically, your pharynx. This tube connects your mouth with your nose and although it can cause problems in the pool, it's very important when it comes to eating. Without it, we wouldn't be able to really enjoy the taste of our food. The taste buds on our tongue can only register sweet, sour, salty, bitter and umami, which is a Japanese word that roughly means "savoury". If those five flavours were all we had, mealtimes would be just as dull and bland as your food tastes when you've got a cold.

Vanilla, strawberry, cinnamon, peppermint and every other delicious flavour you can think of only become real to us when the molecules carrying the smell of the food we're chewing waft up through the pharynx and into our nose. Once there, the molecules insert themselves into passing sensory cells (olfactory receptor neurons) like keys into a lock. The right key can activate the cell, which will pass its information on to other neurons. The next thing we know, we're tasting something that's really only a smell. Because colds tend to block your nose, they close the door to the tastes that make your food so interesting.

GUT FEELING

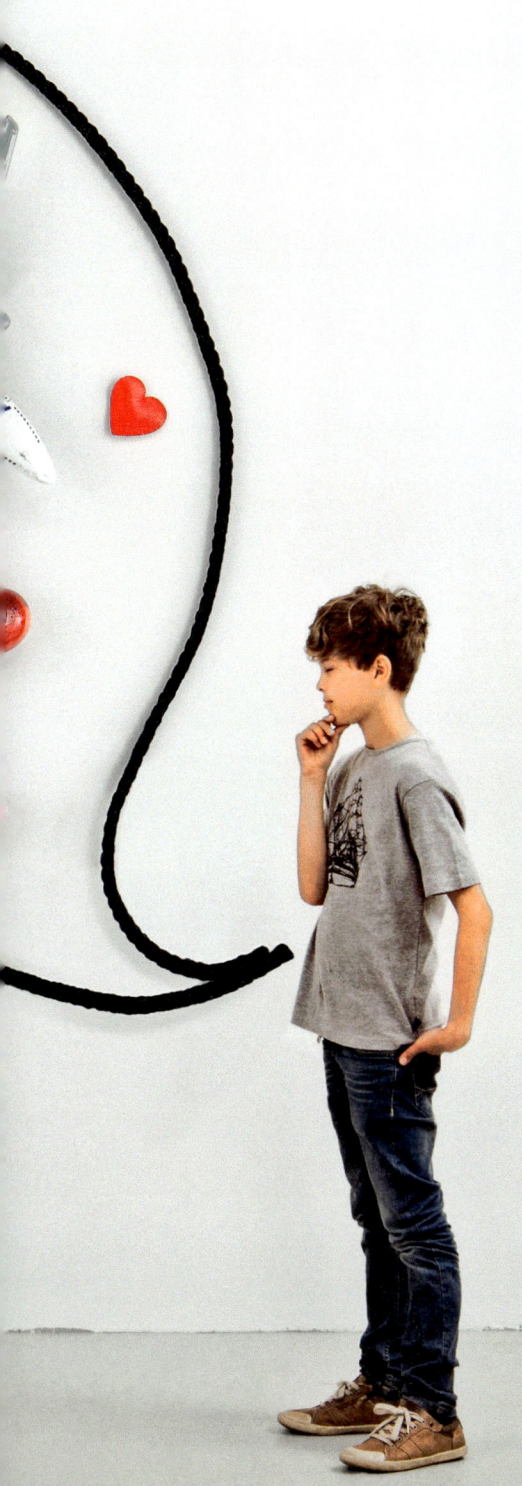

WHEN YOUR BRAIN DOESN'T GET A SAY

What happens when something frightens us?

Life in prehistoric times was dangerous. People had no weapons to fight their enemies with, and no houses to protect themselves from intruders. Every stick could turn out to be a poisonous snake, and every rustle in the bushes could end in death. Luckily, as soon as someone found themselves in one of those situations, their brain would basically go "Ahhhhh!" and then start reacting to the fear. Their hearing and sight would become sharper, and their heartbeat would speed up to make blood rush into their muscles and give them loads of energy. This put the person in the ideal state to either run at top speed in the opposite direction or stick around and fight whatever was hiding in the undergrowth (the technical term for this is the "fight-or-flight response").

All of this helped our distant ancestors survive, and now exactly the same thing happens in your brain when you get scared. You're never actually aware of the processes behind the reaction, as your brain controls lots of body functions and organs automatically and without any need for input from you. But rest assured that if you sense danger, your brain will take over and do its best to get you out of there unscathed.

Does a brain have feelings?

Feelings give life variety and make it interesting. If we didn't have them, we'd all be walking around behaving like robots. Humans can feel loads of different emotions, which is why no single section of the brain is responsible for all of them. Some parts, like the limbic system, have more to do with emotions than others, but it's still not clear whether these parts actually produce emotions or simply connect them up. What's more, a feeling like love doesn't just involve multiple areas of the brain—it also uses lots of different neurotransmitters, which are the chemicals that carry messages across synapses from one neuron to the next. If you've just fallen in love with someone, your brain will be awash with the neurotransmitters that are involved in making you feel happy.

Interestingly, some of the areas of the brain that we use for emotions today were used by our very early ancestors for something completely different: their sense of smell. This is why, compared to other animals, we humans are really good at feeling emotions, but not so hot at smelling smells. It also explains why we often associate smells with emotions, and why people sometimes say "that stinks" if they want to express their dislike for something.

Where does our soul live?

No one knows. Neuroscience and the other sciences can only find out so much. It's impossible for them to prove that the soul exists, so they can't study it to find out where it lives. But just because something can't be proven in a laboratory, that doesn't mean it's not real. Think about things like love, experience and intelligence. You can't see them, but we all know they're part of our world. If scientific evidence had to exist before we could comprehend things, then we wouldn't know much about anything. We'd have no idea how an apple tasted, for instance. So rather than looking to neuroscience for answers about the soul, we all just have to decide for ourselves if it exists and where it might live.

Why do I always start crying when I watch a sad film?

Let's say you're watching a film at home and three things happen: the kid in the film finds his long-lost mother, your brother decides to eat a worm, and your dad cuts his finger while peeling an apple. Chances are, you'll start crying with happiness, pull a face in disgust and (mentally) move your finger out of the path of the knife. It's as if you're the one who's actually experiencing those three events. Weird, right? Maybe, but if we didn't have the ability to put ourselves in other people's shoes and imagine what they're feeling, human kindness and compassion wouldn't exist. Empathy is what makes us hug and comfort a friend when she's in pain. Researchers have studied the way the brain works when we act like this. They looked at people's brains when they hurt themselves, and then made them watch someone they love get hurt. The results showed that the part of the brain responsible for the participants' emotions reacted exactly the same way in both cases.

Not everyone is good at working out how others feel, but the presence or absence of empathy is always reflected in the activity (or lack of it) in just a few areas of the brain.

Incidentally, scientists have found that apes are also capable of empathising. Studies show that the neurons that fire when one ape reaches for a banana also light up when it sees its friend do the same thing. Looking out for others is a pretty good quality to share with a chimp, don't you think?

Is there such thing as a language of emotions?

Kids whose families move to a country where everyone speaks a different language to their own might find it hard to make friends at first. Usually, though, it won't be long before they start communicating quite well without words. One very likely reason for this is that every human (and every great ape) is born with the ability to feel and understand seven basic emotions. We can recognise and interpret the emotions because we all—even children who have never been able to hear or see—communicate them using the same facial expressions. The emotions are happiness, disgust, anger, fear, contempt, sadness and surprise. It has been suggested that other feelings, like pride and love, should also be considered basic emotions, but the jury is still out on that. Basic emotions can appear and disappear very suddenly. The human brain is an expert at recognising them and has developed super-fast connections to process them. This is useful because a basic emotion usually means our body has to take immediate action, like deciding whether to fight or run away. If someone comes at you with anger written all over their face, then your brain has to understand this as a warning and get you out of the way quick.

The facial expressions are also very closely linked to the actual emotions themselves. Whenever your brain tries to work out what someone is feeling by looking at their face, it activates the same areas that allow you to feel the emotions yourself. One way to experience this is to try standing in front of a mirror and smiling at yourself for a bit. There's a good chance that after a few grins you'll actually start to feel happy.

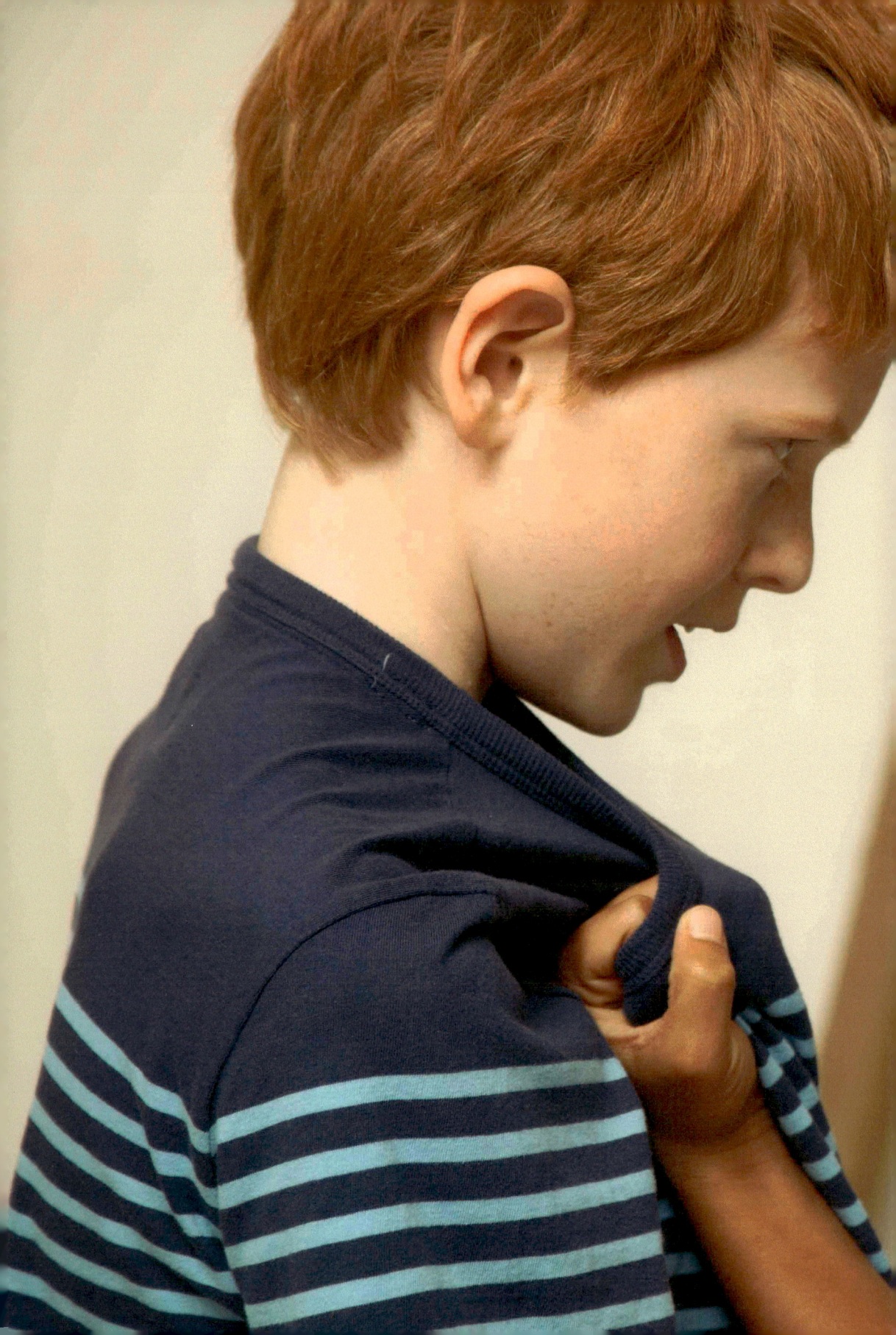

WHAT YOUR BRAIN GETS UP TO AT NIGHT

Does our brain switch itself off at night?

You must be joking! Our brain is such a workaholic that there's no chance of it taking a break while we're asleep. In fact, it's so busy at night that it uses the same amount of energy as it does during the day. All that happens when we nod off is that our brain switches over to different tasks. Some parts become less active, while others work harder. Although we aren't using our sense of sight or hearing, our brain is busy processing the information that it collected during the day. And that's where our (hopefully sweet) dreams come from. Everyone has to sleep, animals included. Scientists studying rats have found that they die if they are deprived of sleep for a few days. As for us humans, if we don't sleep for several days, we start to get headaches and have difficulty concentrating. In the rare cases where someone doesn't sleep for a really, really long time, they begin to lose their mind and will eventually die from organ failure. This shows just how important sleep is for our brain. Although no one really knows exactly why we need to sleep, one very likely explanation is that it gives our brain time to file away the things we learned on one day and to prepare itself for more learning the next. Imagine it like a whiteboard. Once your teacher has filled it up with notes, he has to wait for you to copy them down before he can wipe the board clean and start adding new information.

How can dolphins sleep underwater?

Good question. Sleeping is a problem for dolphins because they're mammals. That means they breathe the same way we do—with lungs—and have to keep coming to the surface for air. If a dolphin (or a whale, or a porpoise) were to stretch out at the bottom of the ocean for a snooze, it would drown. Nevertheless, dolphins, whales and porpoises all manage to sleep as much as eight to ten hours a night. How on earth does that work? With a really neat trick, as it turns out: they only ever sleep with one half of their brain. While one side is resting, the other side stays alert and makes sure the dolphin keeps going to the surface for air. The roles usually reverse after an hour or so, which means the dolphin ends up with a fully rested brain. Marine mammals aren't the only ones to use the trick. Swifts, for instance, also sleep half and half because they spend almost their entire lives in the air.

Can you stop yourself thinking?

That depends on what you mean by thinking. Psychologists and philosophers often define it in a different way to neuroscientists, and even they don't agree on what it means. If we say that thinking happens every time the brain weighs one piece of information up against another and produces a result, then our brain is thinking all the time and there's nothing we can do to stop it. That's because a lot of the tasks the brain performs have to keep going so that we can stay alive. However, if we define it as the steps we take to become consciously aware of a result, then it is possible to stop thinking.

When Buddhist monks meditate, they're trying to switch off this kind of thought. To empty their mind, they might concentrate on their heartbeat or on the idea of not thinking anything. This helps them reach a state where they stop being consciously aware of things. Think of it like being asleep and unbelievably wide awake at the same time. Interestingly, studies have found that meditation makes the monks' neurons begin firing all together in a regular rhythm.

Is it better to study the night before a test, or get a good sleep?

We've all sat there the night before a test and thought: "No time for sleep, I have to read everything all over again!" We're gripped by the fear that the one thing we didn't read will come up and we'll be done for. But even though it might soothe your troubled mind to study late into the night, it's actually not such a good idea. Sleep helps your body and brain recuperate from the stresses of the day and, most importantly, gives your brain time to take everything you've learned and fix it firmly in your memory. So the best way to make sure you can recall your study notes when it really matters is to try and get a good, long sleep the night before. Also, if you arrive at school after studying from dusk to dawn, you'll be exhausted and will find it hard to concentrate. That's not exactly the best state to be in for a test.

What's sleepwalking?

So this girl wakes up and goes down to breakfast thinking it's a normal day. But before she's had time to pour her cereal, her parents start telling her about how she was wandering around the house last night. The weird thing is, she's got no idea what they're on about. If that sounds like a familiar situation, then don't worry, it's totally normal. Loads of kids and teenagers sleepwalk. Some actually get up and walk around, while others just sit up in bed and babble a bit before lying back down again. It usually happens just after they've fallen asleep. In this state, our body is normally at rest. Our breathing and heartbeat have slowed and our muscles are relaxed. With sleepwalkers, though, it seems that the mechanism that switches the muscles off during sleep isn't working properly. If chains of neurons responsible for a particular movement are activated, then their body will perform the movement even though they're not awake. Most people find that their nightly wanderings stop once puberty is over and their brain has reached full maturity.

We are very grateful to the outstanding Hertie Foundation for agreeing to collaborate with us on *That's What You Think!* The foundation provided us with over 300 children's questions about the brain, as well as with our two expert authors, Dr Katja Naie and Prof. Michael Madeja.

The Hertie Foundation is a non-profit organisation, and one of the largest foundations in Germany to exist entirely independently of business interests and specific worldviews. Its numerous projects and initiatives focus on preschools, schools, universities, the neurosciences, and professional and family life. Its work is designed to deliver scientifically based, practical approaches to solving the pressing issues that exist in those areas. The foundation also promotes and encourages individual initiatives and inspires people to drive change in their own lives.

The Hertie Foundation is the biggest private funder of brain research in Germany, and the second biggest in Europe. As such, it makes an invaluable contribution to advancing our understanding of neurological diseases and to improving the treatments available. It also runs a German-language website, www.dasGehirn.info, which takes users on a fascinating, interactive journey into the amazing world of the brain.

Its projects for preschools and schools aim to improve equal opportunities in Germany. The foundation's "Starke Schule" (strong schools) programme includes a nationwide competition for schools and an interstate network of further training opportunities for teachers and head teachers.

The authors would like to thank the following people for their efforts in thinking up so many smart, inspiring and eye-opening questions about the brain: Andrea Herzog, Marion Günschmann and the pupils of Thüringer Gemeinschaftsschule Stadtilm; the pupils of Sekundarschule Roitzsch and the pupils of Integrierte Gesamtschule der Stadt Kelsterbach; Carolin von Fumetti, Monika Schumak, Dirk Adé and the pupils of St.-Angela-Schule Königstein; Mark Greweldinger and the pupils of Gymnasium Konz; Ümmü Gülsüm Özdemir and the pupils of Clemens-Brentano-Europaschule in Lollar; and the Hertie Foundation's Starke Schule network. Our thanks also go to Prof. Michael Frotscher and Prof. Denise Manahan-Vaughan for stepping in with their neuroscientific expertise when we reached a dead-end or needed an argument settled, to Vera Heinemann and Prof. Helmut Kettenmann for providing us with support from the German Neuroscience Society, to Katharina Ebinger for polishing our texts and being a highly constructive member of the team, and to Marion Bassfeld and Claudia Finke for their outstanding organisational efforts at the Hertie Foundation.

The photographer would like to thank the Vampirklasse at Paula-Fürst Gemeinschaftsschule in Berlin, the Lichtkind Agentur Berlin and the many families who gave their time and inspiration to this project. A special thanks goes to Daniel Neubronner (teacher), Stefanie Kaste (mother), and all the children and their parents. Your trust, your wonderful ideas and your enthusiastic support helped to make this book what it is.

Jan von Holleben was born in Cologne in 1977. He studied special education in Freiburg before traveling to the UK, where he earned a degree in the theory and history of photography at the Surrey Institute of Art and Design in Farnham. After spending seven years in London as an art director, picture editor, and founder of various art and photography organisations, he returned to Germany and now lives in Berlin. Jan works for a number of German publications, including *Geo, Geolino, Die Zeit, Zeit Leo, Spiegel, Dein Spiegel, Neon, Eltern, Chrismon* and *SZ Magazin*. Working on *That's What You Think!* gave him the chance to finally research and understand all his weird and wonderful ideas about the brain.

Michael Madeja was born in 1962 in Detmold, Germany. He is a neuroscientist, a doctor, and a professor at Frankfurt University. He is also one of the directors of the Hertie Foundation, where he oversees the neuroscience and university divisions. Michael has three young children in kindergarten and primary school, enjoys writing books and takes great joy in sharing the mysteries of the brain with children and adults alike.

Katja Naie was born in 1974. She holds a degree in biology and a PhD in neuroscience. Katja is director of www.dasGehirn.info, a website dedicated to the brain. The work allows her to engage with a broad readership and share her fascination for the brain and the role it plays in our feelings, thoughts and actions.
Katja has a five-year-old son who just loves listening to Mum tell him all about the most intriguing organ in the human body.

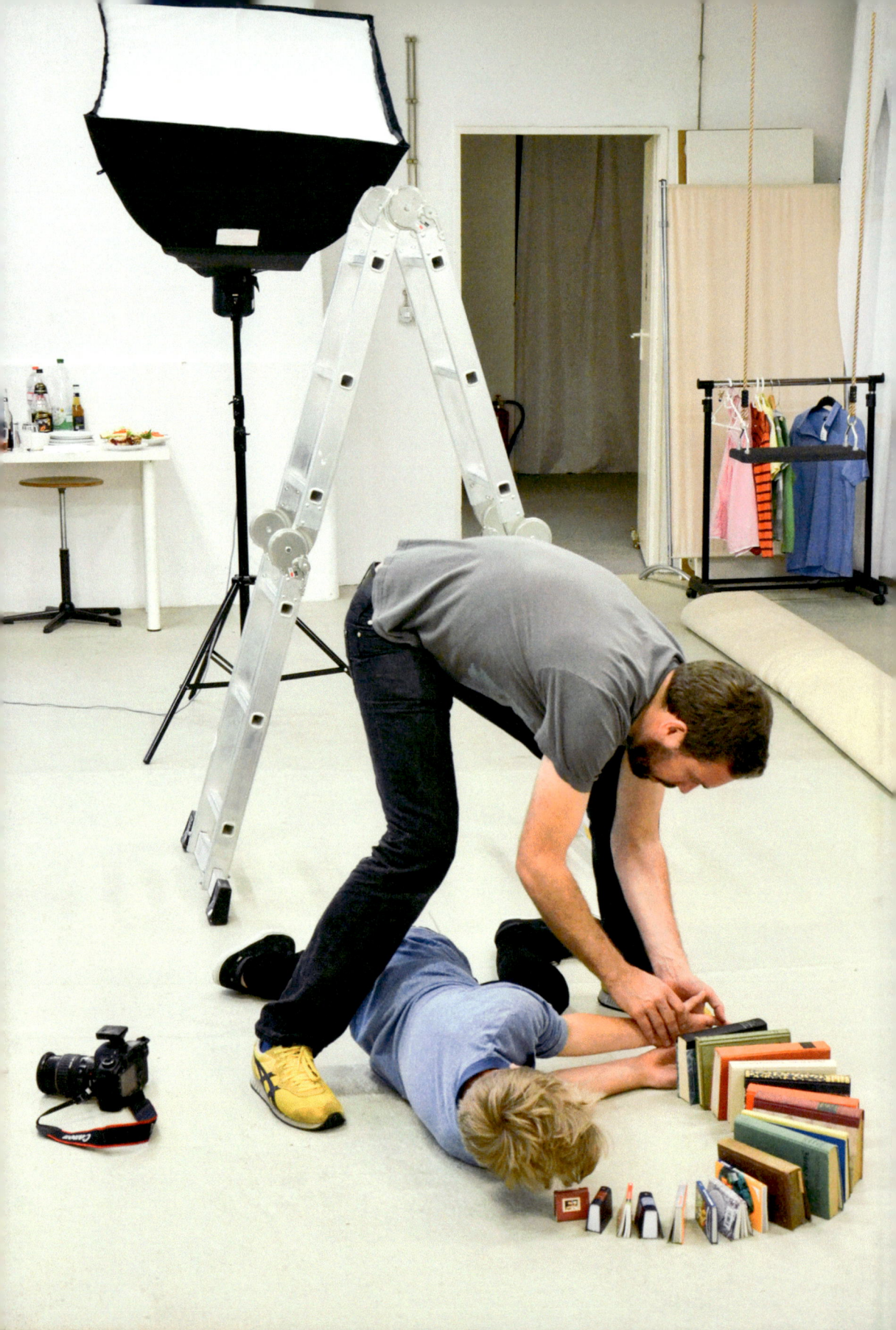

IMPRINT

That's What You Think!
A Mind-Boggling Guide to the Brain

Idea, concept, and photography by
Jan von Holleben
Texts by Michael Madeja and Katja Naie
Questions collected by the Hertie Foundation
Translation from German by Jen Metcalf

Additional layout by Hendrik Hellige
Typefaces: Universe by Adrian Frutiger,
Block Gothic by Steve Jackaman

Published by Little Gestalten, Berlin 2014
ISBN: 978-3-89955-724-4

Printed by Livonia Print, Riga
Made in Europe

The German original edition
Denkste?! Verblüffende Fragen und Antworten rund ums Gehirn was published by Gabriel Verlag.
© for the German original: Gabriel Verlag (Thienemann Verlag GmbH), Stuttgart/Vienna 2013
© for the English edition: Little Gestalten, an imprint of Die Gestalten Verlag GmbH & Co. KG, Berlin 2014

All rights reserved. No part of this publication may be reproduced or transmitted in any form or by any means, electronic or mechanical, including photocopy or any storage and retrieval system, without permission in writing from the publisher.

Respect copyrights, encourage creativity!

For more information, please visit our website www.gestalten.com.

Bibliographic information published by the Deutsche Nationalbibliothek.
The Deutsche Nationalbibliothek lists this publication in the Deutsche Nationalbibliografie; detailed bibliographic data are available online at http://dnb.d-nb.de.

This book was printed on paper certified by the FSC®.

Gestalten is a climate-neutral company. We collaborate with the non-profit carbon offset provider myclimate (www.myclimate.org) to neutralize the company's carbon footprint produced through our worldwide business activities by investing in projects that reduce CO_2 emissions (www.gestalten.com/myclimate).